IN WITH THE OLD, OUT WITH THE NEW

IN WITH THE OLD

OUT WITH THE NEW

Poems by
Jude Lally

Accents Publishing • Lexington, Kentucky • 2021

Printed in the United States of America

Accents Publishing
Editor: Katerina Stoykova
Cover Image: Photo by Lisa Lally

Library of Congress Control Number:
ISBN: 978-1-936628-63-6
First Edition

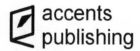

Accents Publishing is an independent press for brilliant voices. For a catalog of current and upcoming titles, please visit us on the Web at

www.accents-publishing.com

CONTENTS

III. Leftovers Warmed Over

I. Tales of Love, Lust and Loss

ADVICE FROM A PLAYER

Success with women is like
success with anything:

it's no secret—
> you never meet successful men
> without hearing all about it.

#1 Be free
   lay it all on the line
   leave everything behind

#2 Be funny
   pitch a line to provoke a smile
   act like it's natural

#3 Confidence is crucial
   quiet is cool
   awkward is the enemy

#4 Play the odds
   plant a lot of seeds
   mix and match

It's bizarre—
> a pessimist thinks all women are bad
> an optimist hopes they are.

ON THE PROWL

One of these days I'm gonna fall off that late-night covet train
    called unjust lust
My foot will be pulled under the wheels of the testosterone caboose
    and you won't even notice I've gone
Seems I'm way down on your line
It won't be pretty at the time
    so keep churning out futile bar tabs

Feeling desperate this Valentine's Day—
    a typical Thursday
What I'd give for a nice warm piece of butternut cream pie
I pass obscene gestures just to get
    to the good part: eye-candy absorption—
    already unwrapped and licked sticky
    by the casual envelopment of confidence
    arising from the primal instincts of the conquer

Sitting in this henless coop
    spines recline around familiar camarilla
Hapless beings on display: a finicky buffet
    affable but resigned to the facts
    confined to pussyfoot onlookers

Until my kindled soul unleashes the beast
    to stomp out this savage wanton imagery
    adhering to these prejudiced Svengali
    dancing on venal strings like worthless sycophants
A marvelous day it will be:
    content with staying home

STREAKS

Envisioning
the opening
has me dripping
quickly sticky,

like a cold container
fresh from 'fridgeration.
I too am wet
with condensation.

As a frosty beverage sweats,
a hot bod perspires
and both
moisten my desire

but a damp spot
left untouched
dries up,
as does lust.

ODE TO THE THREE-YEAR-OLD CONDOM

You thought
your time to unwind
and stretch out
would never come

For a while,
I thought the same

We struggled,
celibate and unused,
to the tune of
34 months, 3 weeks, 4 days and ...
TOO DAMN LONG

Your purpose:

Field fly balls
Shield shooting stars
Gather scattered seeds
Secure spilled *splooge*
Collect unjerked jism

Forgot?
CERTAINLY NOT

a new romance
has bloomed,
so grab a helmet,
you're going in!

A CONVERSATION

A conversation using text messaging

each character

       carefully

              keyed-in

one sentence

       one word

              one letter

       at a time

Back

                  and

forth

                it

went

3

       4

              5

    messages sent

Then

      a break

          in the dialogue

Finally she writes,
"Looks like I'll b
stuc at work
pas midnite 2nite"

         Quickly he taps,
         "Dats alrite,
         we both dserve
         a good nites sleep
         after las nite ☺

RELIEF

for Christin

Relief comes in many forms.
Some find it in a pill,
others, a bottle; others
still, in a satiating drag
or an intoxicating toke.

I find it with My Baby, by
knowing that when shadows
disappear fears of loneliness
are alleviated and when the
weekend sails in like a baffling
fog, she's my lighthouse.

Even when I have no plans
my agenda is already full;
by default, she'll be with me
and I with her, 'cause a man
without a woman is like
a vessel run ashore.

AUTUMN A/C

On a mild night
the late-October sky
cries out for longing
as two lovers embrace

The burning desire between them quickly
sends the woman stumbling fumbling
for the switch which controls
the airflow

This tryst builds
for weeks—

without freeing the
forming bluff
up front

or relieving the
suppressed sensations
of consensual grownups—

so when the couple at last kiss
such impassioned romance ensues
it sets off a series of events:

sparks fly with such
immensity that all the dry
pastures of the world
immediately ignite

whistles blow with such
ferocity that all the fleeing
crooks of the world
stop in their tracks

thunder crashes with such
intensity all the snapping turtles
of the world release their grip

IF MY CLOCK COULD TALK

Stop using me
just to see
what time it is!

Typical male—
all you care about
is getting my digits

Don't you see
I'm not just a
pretty face and arms

I have eyes too,
I see you
looking at other clocks

I'm digital
but I still
get wound up

You keep pushing
my buttons,
I'm liable to go off!

SWEATER WEATHER

Sweater weather
comes along faster
than new love
loses its luster

To keep from
growing cold
one must add
layers of clothes

before fall chills
the air and
old fabrics fray

Likewise,
to fuel the
fires of romance

one must try
new techniques
before tension
sets in

and the first
brisk blast gets
to exposed skin

That's why sweaters
are durable
That's why it's called
making love

THERE IS SOMETHING TO BE SAID

There is something to be said
about waking in the middle of the night
sweating
                    wondering
why the space heater's set so high

        but realizing
rising to regulate the swelter myself
        would likely cause such a fuss
with the sleeping
                    snoring succubus

lying beside me
taking up
                    2/3 of the bed
            that instead of accusing

        her of attempted smother

I simply
                    roll over
                    uncover
and start over

WHO KNEW?

Who knew
electrical plugs
had genders?

The outlets
on walls
are females;

the prongs
at the end
of chords
are males

Who knew
electrical plugs
had ... *genitals!?*

When you stick prongs in outlets
enough times the outlet walls expand
and lose contact with the prongs

And when this happens,
through repeated penetration,
all you can do is
find another outlet
to stick your prong in

So when you find one that fits
                     stick with it!

MAKE ME MAD

Go ahead
make me mad
then I won't be
so damn sad!

Tell me
what we had
meant nothing
to you

Tell me
you can't wait
to meet some
other dude

and that
deep down
you're really
glad

'cause
right now
anger is easier
than despair

THE FLICKERING FLAME

I. Burns through
    wind and rain

    withers over
    pride and shame

    When abrupt gusts
    threaten to blow it out

    it bends backwards
    rekindles callously

II. I wake
     stuffed in a cage

     blindfolded
     both hands bound

     behind my back
     gate locked

     you bear the key
     around your neck

     I plot my escape
     wait for you

     to look away
     still can't go

III. On and on
     off and on

     feelings inflamed
     an engagement in vain

my good name cremated
a love in shame

in spite of other fires
your char remains

APART

This bed   you've made
don't feel   like opening eyes
or putting   feet on floor
only laying   awaiting death

Each day   begins and ends
in a stream   of tears
afraid you'll   never see her again
even the air   is lonesome

You stop   keeping up
with the world   watching tv
going to movies   eating out
get back   to life without

Don't pretend   other friends
will come   see you
your phone   seldom rings
no one   ever knocks

Block talk   break off
pack pipe   pop top
polish craft   pout
carve   yourself out

Accept   she's gone
Continue   move on
Refrain   ringing bell
life's bout   is undecided yet

MORNING STIFFNESS

Upon waking this morning
    I see
    you're up before me

Rise & Shine
    in a whole new light

Standing upright
    like an antsy plaid-covered teepee

Already erect
    as if urging me,

I'm awake before you;
    I beat you, now beat me!

Okay, okay, I say
    You're the boss, hoss!

THE THIRD WHEEL

always rolls through rough terrain
patches of gravel or stretches of high
grass prove no match for its will

when facing thresholds or stumps
it hits with a running start or kicks
it up a notch to get over humps

it never navigates its own path
always follows the other two
no use being alone

CRUSH

for Nelly

I once rose reluctantly
yearning for the one I'd lost

now I rise eager to see
her beautiful smiling face

hear her lovely
wake-up call

inhale her essence
hold her steady embrace

and, lastly, steal a kiss
I must dismiss this notion

for fear of finding it
an unrequited urge

She comes in the morning
goes with a hug

I squeeze softly
breathe her in again

II. The View from Down Here

OPENING UP

Before I begin I'd like to say
if there is something wrong with me
it wasn't always this way and it didn't suddenly appear
out of the clear, blue sky one day.

I don't even begin to know how to tell you what happened to me
but although it didn't "run in the family," somehow it spawned
from my gene pool randomly.

Well I'm not sick, at least not in a contagious sort of way
I don't aim to preach but I've got a lot to say:
my condition isn't cognitive,
my perils aren't simply day-to-day,
my ailment isn't "all in my head,"
It severely hampers movements in my arms and legs
But this disease affects my heart, hearing and my eyes,
in fact, sometimes I can't keep from seeing red.

Now I'm not slow, I just talk that way.
I need people to comprehend, not just get the gist of what I say.
I know what you're thinking, and the answer is NO,
I haven't been drinking.
I know I slur my words sometimes so it may seem that way.

Let me put it like this: don't be so bold as to ask
"What's the matter with me?"
Put it in another way, perhaps a little more delicately.
At least I'm not paralyzed, the jewels still illuminate lustrously
they're just not in high demand.
Just don't expect me to wiggle my big toe,
and—*for God's sake!*—find someone else to lend you a hand.

ATAXIA

Literally, it means loss of the ability to coordinate muscle movements
It refers to any of the symptoms of a neurological disorder.
In the medical world it means uncoordination resulting from brain
  damage
In my world it is not quite so well-defined.

To me the ataxia is undeniably what's attacking me, although, it's hard
  to acknowledge the ubiquitous activity.
But it's not like a blitzkrieg attack—occurring suddenly and with
  constant heavy bombardment, although, the *"attack of me"* does
  occur constantly ... and as far as we know, without remedy.

No, this disease that's constantly and relentlessly *"attacking me"* – the
  ataxia – is more like
  the tortoise in *The Tortoise and the Hare,* slow and steady, but
  persistent, and in the end victorious.
But unfortunately this ataxia, that is simultaneously *"attacking me"*—all
  of my externalities—knows no sense of the word, VICTORY ... to
  me, though, there's only pressing on.

My ataxia is degenerative, which means it'll get worse and worse.
So when people ask me, "Well, what's the prognosis?"
All I can do is grin, wide-eyed and say, "Just one day at a time."
Maybe a mighty wind will come along and flip that old tortoise upside
  down.

Then there's Charlotte, a 45-year old barfly I see quite a bit at the pub.
She knows me and I know her ... She knows about me—my condition—
  but only what she's seen
I told her once its progressive; she said, "I've known you for a year and I
  haven't noticed any change."
But that was right before I turned to wheel home and she kissed me
  lasciviously and uttered, *"I love you."*
I promise I didn't tell her as part of my condition, I developed
  elephantitis of the penis.

Another time, an older lady indelicately asked me: "What's *wrong* with you anyway?"

I smirked and said, "Besides being young and handsome, yet still single … I don't know what you mean?"

Then there was my dad, who said, "In two more years, you won't even be able to get out of the house on your own!"

He was probably just upset with my obstinacy.

If I believed that, then the tortoise has already crossed the finish line.

Maybe a tractor-trailer will come barreling along the course and whirl that tortoise around in the opposite direction.

INDECISIVE INSIGHT

Under hovering showers of joy
This assistance presence is felt
Adorn time forgot names brushed gingerly
Compelled to feel awkwardly, somberly

Everyone always seems to have something else going on
Flares and smoke signals ought to be available upon request

Photo booths and airplane bathrooms are unlikely candidates
Standing ovations
Some movie theaters with stadium seating cause strain in necks
Haunted footing on inclines of mirrored houses for freak shows

Underneath there is no camouflage
On the inside there is still hemorrhaging
From far away this sturdy paper plate may look soiled
Probably all the exterior labels need relaminating
But catch me on a good day and you'll find all smiles.

TRY

Try to rise each day with only intentions:
>no said date, no timeframe, no deadline
only aim expression, spilling impressions

Try to put on a happy face
>hold head high, suppress any urge to cry
even though long ago answers passed by and so much
time spent wondering why
>put anguish away
'cause many have worse days

Try to stay healthy
>the longer you can, the longer you'll feel like a man:
doing things on your own, following a game plan, not living in a home
supple and slim, picture yourself weighing 210?
a hefty load making packing grueling, straining backs of friends

Try to make all appointments on time
>even when the unexpected occurs, even when mishaps happen
keep careful eyes on clocks
>'cause an hour session ain't much
no room for error, little lapses collapse quickly
>and the next bus runs in thirty minutes

Try to come up with the next line
>it don't gotta rhyme
hopefully it'll make people take note, it'll make sense
>it'll be something that quiets a noisy crowd or
sends shushes all around
words that'll comfort epileptics in flashing lights,
that'll inspire all walks of life

Try to bear in mind that no one knows exactly what to do
>how to make it work, how to make the
transfer, when to lift, push or pull

better than you … 'cause it's not just dealt with occasionally,
    it's a chronic condition, one that must be
adapted to, one that never goes away

Try to make the most of it
    no matter what hand you're playing with:
small pair, ace of spades
win or lose, who's to say; all that counts is how you play
    you only live once, no time to waste
embrace love, let go of hate

PARKING AT KEENELAND

Arriving late
Combing the parking lot
Hoping for an open spot
Wondered which way to go
The first guy didn't know
Flashing our tag
Necks outstretched
We asked the lady in brown
Like she knew her way around
Pointed past the white van

"Watch the people!"

Slow your roll!
Hold your horses!
"Or we'll need more handicapped spaces."

TRAGIC

No trying to hide
Handicap pride
Smooth in stride
although rounding-off edges
scraping paint jobs
and murdering flip-flops—oh my—
why can't every doorway be three feet wide?
What an eyesore
Aspiring to be
a traveling writer some day
Trounce the earth
Lay
Say, "Hey!
How would you feel!?"
Coming apart at the seams
of age now realizing different dreams
The last person you want to be is no one
Lost track of the definition of fun
June's coming enjoy the sun
But for now, take the casualties as they come

THE DAILY GRIND

Proving nothing but spite
Awaken break of daylight
To the sound of children screaming
Realizing—it's beyond dawn—*I'm dreaming*
Time spends on a dime
Apparently, it's recess time
And here, lying all exposed
Cacophony coming in through the window

Decided that getting used to this was enough
Ruling the world is tough facing rough stuff
What it takes is guts
Get a hold of yourself and stop pulling stunts
Start paying the rent by the 3rd of each month
Get over to the park
Get a tan
Get sane
Do whatever you got to do

Imagine waking with an agenda
With an early start time
With a *real* morning
Rushing for the door
Many odious to do's
Boohoo

Dealing for the future while fighting
Searching for the old man within
Must be treasure at the end of the rainbow
Fed up waiting for my time to shine
Starving and unfulfilled frame of reference
Diagnosed ten years gone sour preference

Now I travel with fate unknown
Caught between the drapes of life
Now is the time to write

GRAVITY

Up: in the air, in the chair, in my lap, in the clasp of my hand.
Down: to the ground, beyond my reach, between these feet, beneath
    this seat.
So quickly things fall below me—
Well, it's not supernatural … It's just *GRAVITY.*

Gravity—When all I wanted was to stay awake, you weighed on
my eyelids like some unwanted blindfold, *as if*—I needed to be told,
"Bedtime, lights out I say!"

Gravity—You wouldn't let the boxer rise to finish the fight—too bad;
10 count in the 9th. Your aim is to get the best of people. You drag them
down even when they've turned their lives around. That *ain't* nice!
What gives *you* the right?

Gravity—You're the reason toothpaste dribbles down my chin onto
my crotch after I've already dressed and am headed for the door. Now
I gotta face the daunting task of changing pants. Thanks a lot, now I'll
never make my escape.

Gravity—You keep me bending, you keep me reaching, you keep me
doubled over. I've done many a face dive because of you, right to the
floor, suffered rug burn on my forehead, rolled out of bed, hit the deck,
took a spill, tested my will.

Gravity—You asshole, remember that night when I came home with ol'
what's-her-name and we were so close to bed but without my strap on I
succumbed to the floor instead. Well I've fixed that now at least; started
wearing my seatbelt everywhere.

Gravity—A million times my book fell, my Discman dropped, the
batteries lost. Could you delay me any more? How many times will you
make me rinse off my silverware? Spilled drinks, overturned ashtrays,
dinner-go-plop—WHAT THE HELL?—do you *really* think I can operate a
mop?

Gravity—You sick son-of-a-bitch, always taking up all my time. Whether you're swallowing my cell phone, making off with my money or causing the arching of my spine, you always keep this smile in decline.

Gravity—What purpose do you serve anyway? Without you things would always stay right up in the air, and guess what?—that's how I like it. So sometimes I wish you'd just stay the fuck away from me!

I can't stress enough the **gravity** of the situation.

SWIMMING

When I'm swimming
I'm all business
Don't even try to talk to me
   when I'm swimming
Concentrating on
   staying in rhythm—
      stoke, breathe in
      arms in, let it out
All the way down
Then once I'm at
   the shallow end,
   standing and reclining
   then headed back again.

When I'm swimming
   most likely I'm counting—
   always keeping tabs
   on the number of laps
Or looking up at the clock
Wondering how I'm doing ...
   when the ride's coming

Mostly my eyes stay down though—
   focused on that big bold black line
   on the bottom.
Unless I catch a glimpse
   of some tight thigh walking by

Perhaps I'm reciting
   the Presidential Rhyme
   from eighth grade:
"Wash, Ad, Jeff, Mad, Mon, Ad, Jack, Van Har, Ty, Po, Tay, Fil, Pierce,
   Buke, Con ..."
         It *gets fuzzy after Lincoln:*
Or, maybe I'm singing the state song:

"Alabama, Alaska, Arizona, Arkansas, California, Colorado,
   Connecticut..."
  not knowing "My Old Kentucky Home"
Or, I could be constructing a poem
Either way, it's tiring
  yet invigorating,
  confining yet liberating
It makes me feel free
cause in the pool
  it's flowing and moving
  and ... it's all me

THINGS COULD BE WORSE

You can never wish the world away.
You can only wish it here to stay.
You do not realize who's the one to blame.
Carry the burden.
Blare out the presence
and perceive one moment that life
isn't to be lived in vain.
Suppose that things could be the way they used to be.
Standing and learning the sort of things a person's
supposed to see.
Watch how much faster time goes by
now that you're on your own.
Look at all these children
know that they're all watching you.
Catch a case of the willies
thinking about the way things are going to end up.
Realize the answer
a little too late to negate the time spent on growing
up
and finding out there isn't a Savior ...
'til you're dead and gone.
There's nothing better than to wake up
to someone bringing you water.
Or to hear a familiar knock on the door
when you're all alone and it's getting dark out.
But the summer nights are warm and long
so you can stay out late.
When you know the answer lies
on the inside of this lovely mind
all you gotta do is get it out.

Tomorrow's the final day
to put the down payment on the house.
Check out the exposure on the reel;

alas, someone's got to keep their composure
even in the face of perilous danger.
Things are easier to deal with now
that you don't have to scurry and worry
about what you always aspired to be—
envisioned being free.
So just sit back and imagine
exactly what it feels like over here
with this mind and this body—
having this mental capacity
lacking basic ability.
Hold on, it's not all cantankerous:
the fact of the matter is
my existence is marvelous.
I can spend all day in pants that I wake up in.
I never rise to the interrupting—
rude awakening, recurring buzzing—
of an alarm clock.
Nor do I have to shave but every eight days
or bathe every day either
for that matter.
Hey, things could be worse:
I could be living with this curse since birth
but since I had, at least, a normal childhood
I can veil most of this melancholy.
I possess a stoic mentality
not exhibiting most of this hostility
'cause things could be *much* worse.
At least I still know how to party.

I've been known to recite a certain mantra—
of late it's more like an affirmation, a realization,
a philosophy for living in this building.
So if you'll indulge me for one second longer—

it goes like this:
It is better to be alive than to be dead and gone
or to have never been—
never conceived through original sin.
So when you put it that way—
when you live like today could be your last day
it sure makes things easier to deal with.
Life will be
but an adventure can induce fun.
A day in the sun is better than a day
spent in some office
dealing with the public
or on some time line
trying to meet the deadline.

SIDEWALKS

                        Sidewalks can be tricky sometimes
Oftentimes they're littered
        with trash cans, recycling bins, old furniture or worn-out appliances
            like bathtubs, water heaters, 'fridgerators, stoves, and toilet bowls
                        making passing a hassle,
                            it can be damn near impossible!

What I hate most is when they're built
        without a tilt down to the street
            like the roadway engineers
                didn't stop and think
                    and certainly didn't
                        complete the design
                            with the disabled in mind

The problem may be structural damage
            due to tectonic or temperature shifts
Cracks   Gaps   Uneven slabs   No one keeping tabs

There may be too big a bump,
                too deep a dip,
                    too wide a trench
                            between cement seams,
too narrow,
        too worn down,
                too beat up,
                        or too dangerous all around
blocks may be missing,
        torn up for construction,
            left in *reconstruction*,
                causing mobile obstruction
                        and circled off with yellow police tape saying
                        DO NOT CROSS!

but in a wheelchair it's impossible to step off, so you:
    try navigating around,
        cutting through the grass or rubbing against a wall
            teetering a ditch or maybe even rolling right out into the street—
                IT'S TRECHEROUS, *IT'S A REAL BITCH!*,

so you turn around and go back the way you came,
        and you backtrack a tad (hopefully)
            then you gotta find an alternate route,
                    now you're running late … and because of that,

you might have to rush to get back on track,
                        you may be more willing to take chances
you might risk being injured or run down,
                    all because you had to find another way around

        But between these two scenarios, it's usually the latter,
            and you wind up feeling like your well-being doesn't matter.

NOVEMBER NATURE "WALK"

It was a short walk
            out to the top
                        of Chimney Rock today—
but it was not
          without symbolic attainment
                        nor nostalgic benefit

It was long enough
          to trigger recollections
                        of pastimes spent
in that marvelous wilderness
          when we kids ruled those woods

and when it wasn't
          such a spectacle
                        straying from the path—
          when, in fact,
                  we made our *own* path.

It was somewhat chilly
                in that cool, crisp autumn air
all the wildlife were missing
                    all the treetops were bare
but maybe it was just me
          who thought it was nippy—
all the while sitting
          does little to generate
                  body heat.

Perhaps in my biped days
              this trail would have bored me—
      leading the pack
             would not have fulfilled me—

but now
            just making the trek
                                    is enough
        to spell victory.

AT ODDS

It's been in all the papers
We've heard it on the radio
We've seen it on the TV show

The Woodland Arts Fair

We hear the chatter
We smell the batter
We sense the enormity of the crowd

Here we go!
Walk and roll!

Across Main
Down side streets
Cutting our commute in two
As we draw near
it gets harder to steer
But I'm not worried
I have no fear

Up a stretch of sidewalk
Minding ankles and toes
Wearing my mind out en route
Alas we arrive and it's one big bustle

Where does one begin?
What does one buy?

The Woodland Arts Fair

Where like-minds mingle
and dog-collars jingle
Where friends encounter friends
        and the booths never end

Where jewelers, sculptors and painters
    converge with collectors
Where dollars drop faster than buttons
    pop off
Where only passing through
    entails an apology

Ten 'til two
and I'm due
a gold star
just for coming out

Supporting people's crafts
yet still
trying to figure out my own
But at least
I'm bearing the heat
like everyone else

FALL'S FALLEN SOLDIERS

Dead leaves leave little traction
when walking on stairs,
      when waiting for Winter winds to cease,
    or when transferring into cars from wheelchairs

When one
      is trying to
          keep feet
             from slipping;

            trying to get
      a grip,
    some firm
footing

     on the ground

dead leaves can leave things
            to the laws of motion

CONFINED

My daily functions
and activities,
or lack thereof,
fit with
being somewhat stationary

For instance,
I might get on the couch
and stay glued
to the boob-tube
all day

watching my Wildcats play
or witnessing two good
pro-football teams
collide in primetime,

wishing it was me out there
or at least
hoping that each contest
       comes down to the wire

      ~

Frankly,
I also admit
that I like to sit
in the john
all day

reading novels or newspapers
sending text messages
or rethinking my situation—

usually drinking
two cups of coffee—
while I'm waiting
      on my morning glory

JUST TO GET BY

Approaching swiftly
from down the street, reveling
Winter air nipping
each breath expanding, escaping
Hands covered
joystick *still* shivering

Coming steadily
from street to sidewalk
into parking lot
onto walkway
Invading space gradually
almost stealthily
marking my territory

Smokers take notice
nudge and elbow
stand uptight upright
so I can get by, inside
let greenbacks blow
watch our team's demise
Tonight's enemy
dressed yellow

Outside double-doorway
my patience testing
Waiting to inch in
How many more times
do I need to say it?
Excusing necessary, feeling eluding
Quickly announcing
not only walking
drinking and driving
patting, poking,
unrightfully grab-assing

attention gathering
Step aside enabling
apology accepted
Magazine stands encroaching
approaching frustration

Toes aware
coming through, beware
except for one
Too late!
too much hesitate
not enough dictate
BUMP! SMASH!
up and over
DANCE! RELOCATE!
implicate, shrug and simmer
No hope for surrender
realize, empathize, notice, appreciate
Remember next time
exact moment without indicate

PEDESTRIANS BEWARE

A brief but bitterly wretched commute:
it wasn't without incident though—
nothing ever is when I roll.

On the street,
in the cold,
my pace swift,
dwarfing walking speed.
I was moving too fast then
For the sidewalks.
There was nothing
I could do.
Not an instant to shout,
MOVE! or WATCH OUT!

I nearly barreled over top of him.
Starting at his heel,
running up his calf,
then thigh,
hip,
back,
shoulder—
his upright stance collapsing
from the mass of my unit.

I nearly flattened him,
Embedded his face in the cement,
mashed his head
like a soft pack,
throughout a night of bar hoppin'.
That surely is how it felt

Then it was me,
afraid and apprehensive.
If he had thrown a beer

in my face,
it wouldn't have been
totally unforeseen.
Realizing I deserved
this much at least.

Yet it never happened.
After all,
it had been an accident;
reckless driving—perhaps,
but still a mistake.
Thinking I was moving fine
and having nothing
in front of me.

Perhaps the lapse in judgment
Was his;
not paying attention
was mine.
I bore the guilt.
He had to deal
with the pain.

They don't call me
the *L.A. Clipper*
for nothing.

JUDE

… rose with a piercing pain in his toes
having inadvertently kicked the wall beside his bed
with a direct intensity that made him wonder why
he couldn't maintain voluntary movement in his legs
        all the time.

So already Jude was in a sour mood
because now not only did his heart
seem like an open wound, but he had
to endure scraped skin on his toes, too.

Not to mention the rigors of everyday necessity thus
ensued … You see, ever since the move, Jude
felt substantially subdued—
not being able to do all the things he used to do—
now he had a constant caretaker who
oversaw his every move,
        day in and day out.

But because this was all new to Jude, it
would inevitably take some getting used to.
From getting up and going, taking his meds,
getting fed, until she laid him down in bed.

His helper was there making sure all
went well, and she ensured
that Jude didn't end up on the floor
somewhere. Even when Jude
pooed, she would be close by just in case … so that he
may stay regular, which is
definitely imperative in getting back to normal,
        that's understandable.

Jude also slept and, of course, bathed in
the nude, so with his caretaker always there

rousing and dousing, lifting and lowering,
rinsing and cleansing, Jude was accepting a
new level of humility.

But with this fresh format to Jude's
way of doing, well everything,
came certain undeniable perks: for
instance, Jude loved food—
after all, Jude rhymes with food—and before it was a
chore for him even to make a simple bowl of oatmeal. But now
meals come served
       hot and ready, bathing

with ease, getting dressed is a breeze, all the
hassle is gone from shaving, the hustle and bustle
of going out into the world is no more. Jude is pleased
because he now receives all
the things he genuinely needs.

III. Leftovers Warmed Over

FIRST AND LAST

Stranger: What do you do?
Me: I write.
Stranger: Who do you write for?
Me: Myself.
Stranger: Yourself?
Me: And whoever wants to read it.
Stranger: What do you write?
Me: Poetry mostly.
Stranger: And this is how you make a living?
Me: Not exactly, the living part comes unconditionally.
Stranger: What I meant was, where do you work?
Me: I work from home.
Stranger: So what is your job?
Me: My *job* is to keep on living.
Stranger: To keep on living? What kind of a job is that?
Me: It's a full-time job.
Stranger: Humph. I don't understand.
Me: Neither do I.

WORK

In high school
kids work,
slaving away
for minimum wage
in unsavory grease pits

like Micky-D's, Wendy's, or,
in my case, Arby's, or of course—
the *always* delicious—Taco Bell,

where the smell
lingers until
you take a shower
and wash your clothes,

where work hazards
are everywhere,

and where
the greatest perk
is the free food,

or so you think
at the time

In college
jobs aren't
a whole lot
different—

except
better pay
and greater responsibility,

like working late
on say,

a Tuesday night,
having homework
and class at 8

But the boss—
always the same:

some balding,
overweight, overprivileged,
overindulged, self-righteous
prick—

born into this
superior role,

who works you
to the bone
but the law
stipulates breaks

Now it seems
all your hard work
has ... well,

yet to pay off,

although you
get to pick
your outfit,

tasks are still
mundane and repetitive,
yet somehow,
more competitive;

even so, all eyes watch the clock

until
it's time to go
and

you head home, weary, quick
to declare that you *never*
want to see that place again....

You do the same tomorrow.

ALONE AT LAST

Took a stroll today
    role playing lost ambitions
Monday in the park starts
    creative tradition under silent, quiet conditions
Congested emancipation
    the weekend festival goers—goners

vanished, as if some gratuitous, fictitious magician
whisked away all the ball players, skaters, dog walkers
               merry-go-rounder, swimmers, baby-strollers
          jump-ropers, hopscotchers, Tonka-truck city planners

they're all in remission
    favoring elusive position
freedom working on compositions
    bopping head back & forth
        to jazz musicians

Empty walkways, park benches, picnic tables
               tennis courts and dirt diamonds
    Momma birds' chirps cease slowly, chicks nestle in nests
        Sawdust settles around seesaws, playgrounds become placid
           Reverberation of bouncing basketballs subsides

The only sound now
    the buzzing of high-pressure
sodium street lamps

As nightfall falls
    phone calls remind me that absolute seclusion
is an illusion

SEVERED TIES

Have this pen pal
With the same thing as me
I find her in some cripple magazine
In a post asking for correspondence
Anyone who shares this disease

Writing her with angst and joy
I've never really known another case
Hoping we can share the thrill
Settle for nothing less than something real
But we just don't see eye-to-eye

She is a couple years younger than me
Doesn't seem like she goes anywhere
Lives at home, sheltered, with her parents
They bring her up religious as *hell!*
She is an Alabama queen

She thinks she knows the way
How to make it through each day
I wonder how one could sit content
With all that's unfair and still believe
Must be easy with God in heaven, Adam and Eve

All I had to share were stories and jokes
Wanting simply to be myself
But somehow my language offends her
She isn't amused by my caustic wit
She breaks off all relations ... *oh well*

MOTHER'S ONLY LOVER

No way resembling
    my natural father,
his burly, broad shoulders are
    like a sailor manning a ship
        taking on water.

He works with tools and machinery;
    wakes at dawn—
        morning coffee, cigarette—
skips lunch,
    takes no vacation,
        brings home the bacon.

Mom says,
    he's blue-collar
        all the way,
language and books
    were never his forte.

Education—
    you can shove your Masters
        or your Ph.D.
he hasn't any—
    sweat and elbow grease—
        Wipe your ass with a degree!

Sophistication and culture—
    he wasn't brought up this way.
These aren't attacks
    his heart makes up for
        what his mind lacks.

Their courtship lasts a lifetime,
    Mom wants to be sure—
        maintains trust from afar,
    yearning love remains

You'll never catch him driving a Lexus
        or a four-door Sedan one day,
he's a *"pick-up man,"*
        uses six cylinders to make his way.

He's one of those macho types—
        never sports jewels or fur,
            only tight, faded jeans,
but gotta voice
        that will make
            a lion purr

Watch it,
        he's got Texas-blood in him;
don't double-cross
        or look at his lady
            too long,
                he'll be after you.

He's a simple man: likes
        computer games, fast-food—
            early to bed,
early to rise,
        his teams' colors,
            fade into UK blue

Mom waits twenty-two long years
        to tie the knot again,
            he is there for ten
earning my props.
        I gladly call him pops.

DOCUMENTATION

My head is a fishbowl
 filled with murky water
 a dead goldfish drifts atop
 turned gray from days decay
My mind is a barren wasteland:
 once fertile and original
 as a newborn playwright
 super-saturated with folks galore
Now I'm confined
 to constipated captivity
 free but imprisoned
 able but excluded
 pellucid but misunderstood
 like a fresh strategy for a war
 where victory is infallible

Thoughts seem sterile
 borrowed from dismay
 insipid and irrelevant
Must things go on this way?
 one day: indistinguishable from the next
I'm in a hell of a rut
 dug for me long ago
 before I was one man's hope
 before a mother's soap opera
 turned a stoic boldfaced fever

Feeling dead last
 ousted from the common right
Outspoken and untimely I must be
 denied of the given plight
 still haven't fallen in love
 and in lust very seldom

Not good looking enough?
Too slow to the draw?
Could be the stigma
 clinging to my intrigue
 with angst and despondency
 trickling from truth within
Masked and second-classed
 jobless and erroneous
 are my days besought

SOMETIMES

Sometimes my shoulders sink so low.
Sometimes—MAN—I just don't know.

Sometimes it seems like life's too *long* to figure out what to do.
Sometimes it seems like I forgot what it felt like when I knew.

Sometimes the weekend does me more harm than good.
Sometimes I wish everyone just understood.

Sometimes it's like I'm seeing you for the very first time all over again.
Sometimes even *I* feel like a dirty old man.

Sometimes I get tired of staying up all night.
Sometimes I just wanna … *get laid* or *get in a fight.*

NO MATTER WHAT

No matter what
I do
I just
can't escape
this broken body

this wretched vessel
this doomed lifeboat
that nobody wants
and nobody should be

assigned to, subjected to
especially women and children
whose fate would be demise
to wind up swimming with cinder blocks

sunk, stuck
on the bottom of the sea floor
looking up at life
watching the gulls glide by

in the open blue
they'd be envious
of the living, the breathing
and at night

of the twinkling stars
burning zillions of miles away
their presence disguised
only by daylight

and no signal strong enough
to hear the call for help
for once a body is capsized
the mind is sure to follow

NYC LADY

She's faster than a funeral
on Super Bowl Sunday.
Hotter than a shot of
jalapeño whiskey.
Tougher than
Lucifer's little sister,
but not too tough to
know when enough's
enough

From Kentucky,
her family's only
close in proximity.
An aspiring interior
designer, she ought to be
in the city.
Abusive boyfriends,
too, compel the move.

With smiles spanning
the Brooklyn Bridge,
her marksmanship mentality
and "take no shit from anybody"
attitude, she takes
giant bites
from the Big Apple.

THE DEAL

My beloved Aunt Sherry comes to stay with me
to be my first full-time caregiver. She shows up and
goes to work. First she fixes food then asks, "To drink?"
"Beer," I answer confidently, knowing that this is
her beverage of choice. As she grabs me a bottle of
Icehouse from the fridge her tone seems relieved,
"Now you're talkin' my language," as she cracks
open a can of Keystone Light. We sip from
our brews as she hands me a tuna salad sandwich
with chips. Then back in the kitchen she does
dishes, clears counters, puts cups, plates and bowls
in cabinets. She wipes off stove, sweeps floor, takes
inventory of what I eat by looking through my pantry and
fridge. While I continue eating she takes note of everything
in my apartment: my closet—clothes I hang up—dress
shirts, jackets, coats and khakis; 2 laundry baskets for my
dirty clothes, shoes, a vacuum cleaner, I store various odds and
ends here too. My dresser's where I store most of my clothes—on
my computer table sits my monitor, mouse, keyboard, speakers
and printer. At the foot of my bed is a nightstand which holds
a lamp. In the corner is a queen-size bed; the top of the bed
rests against the far wall, to the right of the bed sits a sofa (this
is Sherry's bed for the next couple months). Past this sits a
Lazy Boy recliner. This short outer wall is filled by a dimmer lamp and
bookshelf; " Wow, have you read all these?" she asks with
amazement. Before I answer I take another gulp of lager, "Most of
them." On the upper level of the shelf sits a wooden 3-drawered box,
which contains about two dozen VHS tapes. "Mind if I check
these out?" she asks already opening one of the drawers.
I know she likes movies, "Be my guest," I say. The back wall
is lined with electronics: one of my shelf speakers lies in the
corner; a DVD tower stands in front of the speaker; then sits
another shelf: on the bottom, all lined up stands a collection of *National
Geographic* magazines, my stereo rests in the middle and atop sits

a combination VCR/DVD player.
My television rests on a furniture piece
with 3 drawers storage space. There sits the other speaker; I have
an octagon-shaped table that duplicates as a liquor cabinet and a
closet that houses my water heater. Then there's the bathroom, first
thing she notices is its missing door; It's pretty basic: just
a tub, a toilet, a sink and lots of grab bars,
very small and simple—there's
not much room to maneuver me so there's not much room to fall.
Then she walks out of the bathroom, looks to her left, checks the
wattage of the bulb in the fixture. I've finished eating and we head
outside for a smoke. We talk a little about mom, and
about mamaw and papaw. Then the daylight turns to dusk, Sherry's
mood sombers. She says she has a deal for me. She says I'm here
for you indefinitely, unless you tell me you don't need me anymore
or if something happens to mom and dad and I'm needed back home.

This is how it begins, she never breaks her word; It was me
who breaks the deal as I decide to complicate my life
even further by having my girlfriend move in. I guess
even deals remain to be broken.

MY MORNING DO

My morning do
is wild;
wild like a fire
that spreads all over,
from the foothills of the Rockies
to the hills of Hollywood dreams,

> but it seems natural,
> no primping or fixing
> with picks or brushes,
> combs or curlers

it stays up too
without gel or hair spray,
like a suck-up's hand
does in the day's
homework discussion

My morning do
is animated,
animated like Saturday-morning cartoons,
like Looney Tunes'

> Daffy Duck
> with his unkempt look,
> feathers frolicking
> or the Tasmanian Devil
> dizzy from spinning,
> fur unfurled and free

My morning do
is messy,

> but It's *So Sexy!*
> she tells me

and to think,
I used to go
to great lengths
to make myself presentable

      but by parting
      and flattening,
      I was only
      hiding and disguising

EXTREME SPECTATOR

Ever try watching
four football games at once?
That's what I do
on Sunday afternoons

So much action
All those yards
So much to follow
All those downs

Surrounded by flat screens
Deafening surround sound
Battles waging in all directions
Inch by nose, settling discretions

Extreme spectator sport
Comprehensive sensory overload
They need to call those
HD TVs, AD-HD TVs

ALL JOKING ASIDE

for Dad

The girl in the sandwich shop
doesn't care how much
pirates pay for earrings—

a buccaneer

or why cannibals
don't eat comedians—

they taste funny.

She's only interested in
the pertinent information:

whether you prefer the Reuben
or club, with provolone
or Swiss, on white or wheat.

The same goes for social workers,
desk clerks, valet parkers, waitresses
hair dressers,

the postman, cable guy, lady at the
bank, bakery, dry cleaners, the
freckle-faced kid in the
drive-thru window....

They're there to serve you—
that's *all*,
not to laugh at your jokes
or at *you*, I imagine.

Having heard these
hundreds of times,
I never laugh

but I did when
you told one at
the Japanese restaurant—

What did the catfish say
when he swam into a wall?

Dam!

—I laughed at the
confusion it caused.

Sometimes the ice
is best left intact.

COLD HOUSE

I hate to wake
with frosty feet
and icy toes
numb knees
and chattering teeth

Nothing's worse

I'd rather give birth
to a full-grown grizzly
with no epidural
or be shot in the ass
with a blast
of kindling cosmic matter

Okay that's a little extreme
but I would rather
wait on a gimpy waitress
to finish filling my order
than wrestle the wrath of winter
at aurora

Sometimes, though, it's unavoidable

so when I must
I rush and uncover
dart from my slumber
prance through the parlor
and land legs first
in a steaming tub
of running water

Ahhh ...
nothing warms me
when the house is cold
like a hot bath

LEFTOVERS

Sitting, sifting
through old poems
it occurs to me

that these pages
are akin to the
contents of a deep-

freeze: frozen
fresh for retrieval.
Snapshots of

living legacy,
ready to be thawed
and enjoyed later

without losing
initial flavor. Though
memories have gone

cold they wait
to be pulled out,
reheated, re-served, retold.

THE LITTLE ONE

for Tesse

The little one knows little
but is eager to discover
life's mysteries
as they unfold
and those of the world
still fresh, shrouds of wonder
she tries to see firsthand
rather than rely on what she's told
(she rarely listens).

The little one scampers in unannounced
curious to see what I'm doing
quick to emulate my actions
pressing buttons on my keyboard,
phone, and mp3 player.

"I like this room," she says,
grabbing the bars hanging above my bed
they're good for swinging,
"for monkeying upside down,"
She exclaims, kicking her feet
up, until a slip relegates:
SUPERVISED PLAY ONLY.

She's wild like fire
engulfing the entire place
never taught not to run in the house,
she spreads from room to room
in full sprint, as fast
as her little legs will allow
and I smile, knowing
I will miss her when she goes,
goes and grows up.

A SLUMP

Been in a slump—
down in the dumps,
not really sick-sick
with measles or mumps
just *feeling verklempt* …

losing my voice—
not my voice, voice *literally*
rather, my *literary* voice:
my writing voice, spoken-word voice,
open-mic voice, my *sharing* voice

because *sharing is caring,* I know
but everything takes time—a lot
of time, especially for me—and
there's only so much, thus, I'm going
to climb out of this idle stint so

I must make time to write—even if
it takes all night, even if that's all
I do—because *that's what I do*
I need it, I need it like a DJ needs
airplay, like a doctor needs a

Ph.D., like cops need probable
cause, like farmers need the
rain and—*sure*—we all need
the rain but I could argue that
we all need to write too.

A MENTAL MISFIRE

Me and my old lady been together
fifteen months. I think she is the one

and by *the one* you know which one
I mean. The one I'm going to spend the rest

of my life with; the one that's gonna settle
me down and make me forget all the other

women in the world; the one I'll grow
old with, love to the bitter end, till death

do us part. Now when I say *old lady,* I
mean OLD LADY, literally, she's

nearly twice my age anyway. So growing old
together is never a possibility; guess I

shoulda said: "The one I'll *age* with." Course
who knows how long that's gonna be; neither me

nor anyone else knows what age they'll be
when their number's called. Only God knows.

All I know is, she proves to me that maturity's
got nothing to do with age. It isn't long

after our courting begins that I begin to
realize that she wants the rest of our lives

to be *right then,* and in retrospect, I guess
I'm the one to misconstrue the two.

And anyway, till death do us part is
another one of those not-to-be-taken-literallys.

Parting, like *parting ways* has a connotation
of finality; spending time apart, though,

is only temporary, in fact, it's healthy!
But explaining this to her

is like talking to the broad side
of a barn. Any time I go somewhere it

is like I break her heart,
for real break her heart, like I am

leaving her for someone else. So when
I'm gonna be away a few days I

go through the same old rigmarole. It is
like dealing with a fifty-something-year-old fifteen-

year-old Lordy B, frantic tantrums of insecurity!
Alright now, allow me to offer a preemptive

apology for any innocent ears out there:
It is her pussy power that compels

me to stay. I could dance a ditty
not having to worry about unplanned

pregnancy. But the last straw comes when
she tries to make me forget all the other

women in the world, including my own kin!
Because family runs deeper than blood,

I have to choose between the two. So I say
HELL NO, you gotta go! Now that, I presume,

is the end. But between me, you and the
fencepost, I gotta half-a-mind to go call her again.

WHILE ON HOLD

The expected wait time to speak with an agent
comes and goes like the summer I spend
hoping a heated romance comes along.

Tick-tock, tick-tock goes the clock on the wall;
flip-flop, flip-flop go the pages on the calendar
as the months fall into fall like dying leaves in
an adamant autumn breeze.

I make mental notes: the call volume is highest
earlier in the week and most of this information
can be found at the website of which I shall not
name; for that is not what this poem is about.

Maybe I need to remind myself that love isn't
everything. But it is something—a curse and
a blessing. It's like money: you don't think
it's essential 'til you don't have any.

As for me, I'm an anomaly: I've never had much
money, but it's still not that important to me. I'll
hold while you try and figure that one out.

CONFLUENCE

The last time my father goes to the doctor prior to his death, the doctor asks, "So Mike, how are you feeling?" Dad's answer is a little unorthodox, he says he grew up in Paducah, which is right on the river. It's at a point where two rivers—the Tennessee and the Ohio—come together. After their confluence, one can plainly distinguish—for about a mile downstream—between the Ohio, the far side, which is dirty, brown and muddy, and the Tennessee side, which looks much cleaner.

Meanwhile my stepmom, Cathy, judging by the content of Dad's reply, thinks, What the hell is he talking about? Given his frequent episodes of dementia and his recent diagnoses of Alzheimer's, it isn't uncommon for him to go off on some random tangent.

Dad's doctor has a clear frame of reference into what he is talking about; apparently the Doc's wife is from Paducah so once when they were there visiting, he'd gone to the riverfront and seen firsthand where the rivers join up and the remarkable difference you see in hue as they flow side-by-side until they become one. Having explained this, the doctor says, "Yeah Mike, I know exactly where you mean." Then Dad says, I feel like I'm down in the muddy side.

MY TIME

Lessons to be learned
Brought to breaking point
Crammed with eons of bloody coloring books
Filled and fastened by eternal Godsends

Left behind on a dozen childhood playgrounds
Sent home in the shade alone
Left out to dry by morning bus drivers
and nightly empty driveways

In my time of youth
I'd walk home from school
but only when it was right across the street
Playing the pool hall
Playing the goofball
Running smiles wild
Fixed on females
Ditching school in 8th grade
'cause my girlfriend wouldn't be back
'til after Spring Break
Playing my parent

In my time of growth
the mitochondria slowed production of a protein
No one knows 'cause no one knows
no history of the ailment in the family
Home wasn't the place to be
'cause it was *the* place to be
but when mother hen's away
we chicks played
The fun stopped before it really even began
Friends cringed at the approach
of two mangy full-breeds

In my time of mourning
I felt lost and confused
so I dealt with the loss any way I could
I'd lose myself in books and music,
movies and madness
I'd sit up all night
and write my time away
'till first light
And—yes—sometimes I'd cry
unable to keep my tears
from forming salty cheek streams
Unable to hold onto memories and thoughts
long enough to type

In my time of living
the excitement of finding a source
of happiness grew as long
as lonesome highways of wanderlust
The search for stories to tell
was better than actually getting there
Without a sense of some place to go
my mind threw fits
as my body played tricks
When I met my baby
at last I felt alive
I finally learned to forget
all the things I missed

In my time of dying
I'll leave behind a legacy of love
I'll believe that we make our own peace
When the passage of time has ceased
new chapters open
as old ones close

New fish come and go
Ground is broken
so new gardens can grow

ACKNOWLEDGMENTS

The author would like to express his gratitude to the following individuals for helping make this book possible:

Caregivers & Assistants
> Aunt Sherry Perry
>
> Steve Wise
>
> Khadija Hussein
>
> Tyren Armstrong

Former Girlfriends (thanks for the inspiration)
> E. C.
>
> L. R.
>
> T. G.

Family
> Uncle Jim Lally
>
> Mom Lisa Lally—my most avid fan of all

Special Thanks To
> Katerina Stoykova & the Poezia Writers' Group
>
> Eric Scott Sutherland & the Holler Poet Series

ABOUT THE AUTHOR

Determination has always been Jude Lally's middle name. Whether on the Little League baseball field in elementary school, on the football gridiron in middle school or on the wrestling mat in high school, he always gave it his all. But halfway through high school, at the age of 16, Jude was handed his biggest challenge of all when he was diagnosed with a rare genetic degenerative progressive neuromuscular disease called Friedreich's Ataxia. Daily living as he had known it changed forever. There were new obstacles to overcome, and overcome he did, as two years later he became a proud high school graduate. But he didn't stop there. Five years later he also became a college graduate when he received a B.A. in Business Administration from the University of Kentucky.

But as reality set in and the likelihood of landing a job seemed out of reach. Jude turned to his love of writing to help him cope. While talking about his struggles didn't come easy for him, writing about them did. He cultivated that need to write by joining a writers' group that met weekly in Lexington, Kentucky. That's where he met his future publisher Katerina Stoykova of Accents Publishing.

In With the Old Out With the New is Jude's third collection of poems published by Accents Publishing. As in *The View From Down Here*, published in 2010, and *I'm Fine But Thanks for Asking*, published in 2012, Jude's unique way with words, combined with a sprinkling of Irish wit passed down from his late father, will have you both laughing and crying at the same time if you're not careful! One of Jude's favorite sayings is "The last person you want to be is no one." Being able to share his thoughts and words not only makes him feel like someone but is also a way to shine the light on disabilities and those living with them every day.

Jude currently lives with his Mom and Stepdad near Nashville, Tennessee.

CPSIA information can be obtained
at www.ICGtesting.com
Printed in the USA
LVHW030139100221
678884LV00007B/613